Collected Lyrics and Epigrams

Drama

The Fatal French Dentist (1967)
The Collected Plays, in two volumes (1970-1971)
The Patriots of Nantucket: a Romantic Comedy of the
  American Revolution (1976)
Amphitryon, after Molière (1977)

Poetry

Simplicities (1974)

Fiction

Chi Po and the Sorcerer (1964)
The Gobble-Up Stories (1967)

Critical Translations and Anthologies

The Theater of Don Juan (1963)
Seven Comedies by Marivaux (1968)
Five Comedies of Medieval France (1970)
Three Classic Don Juan Plays (1971)
The Land of Upside Down by Ludwig Tieck (1978)
The Ariadne of Thomas Corneille (1981)
Philoctetes and the Fall of Troy (1981)

Others

A Definition of Tragedy (1961)
Annotations to Vanity Fair (1981)

Oscar Mandel

Collected Lyrics
and Epigrams

ILLUMINATI
LOS ANGELES

For information and permissions, write ILLUMINATI, 1147 South Robertson Blvd., Los Angeles, California 90035.

Library of Congress Cataloging in Publication Data

Mandel, Oscar.
    Collected lyrics and epigrams.

    I. Title.
PS3563. A44A17   1981   811'.54   81-410
ISBN 0-89807-025-2   AACRI

Printed in the United States of America

Aquí hago despedida
que juri a Dios en mi vida
ne me vean más trobar,
en veras ni por burlar.

—*Juan del Encina*

CONTENTS

POEMS AFTER

THE POET

Preface

This volume includes all the poems I care to preserve from approximately thirty years of composition; those I feel I can send without impropriety into a world curiously brimming with excellent verse.

Some have made previous appearances, either in periodicals or in my *Simplicities*, a small collection published in 1974. Others are printed here for the first time. Most, whether published before or not, have been mended and amended repeatedly over the years, and once again for this present and final occasion. Underneath the revisions, however, signs of advancing time remain, and it will be rightly understood that the juicier effusions tend to be cries out of my youth, and the drier verse the effect, by and large, of irreversible maturity. Time is also marked here and there by an inception date attached to a poem. But all in all, a chronological ordering would have been delusive, and I have not tried to impose one.

Instead, I have regimented the poems, regardless of their birthdates, under six chapter headings, and I have even traced, where possible, a faint itinerary within each chapter. Nothing strict is intended. But neither are these categories forced on the poems. As I have been driven to my writing pad again and again, all along the years, by a finite number of concerns, a little shaking, at the end of three decades, sorted out most of the poems with a modest degree of neatness, which translated itself into the six chapters already mentioned.

This is not to confess that six chapter headings exhaust me. Even these loose ones, under which a variety of notions bestir themselves, do not exhaust me; for, looking back, I notice that certain stirrings of mine never allowed themselves to become poems at all. They robed themselves instead in the plays, the fables, and the essays which have taken up much of my "literary energy". Others, naturally, managed to make themselves at home in prose and verse alike. But some peremptorily required poetry for whatever it is that poetry offers:

concentration? music? intensity? or the opportunity, sanctioned by tradition, of talking up a storm about oneself? Mine are — so much is certain — "songs of myself", but I must specify: songs about some portions of myself and not others; and (needless to say) a myself which claims no romantic exclusivity, for a poet is a beast of the tribe like all the rest.

If early and late are made good neighbors in this book, so are — under each of the headings — contrary moods and notions, grave considerations and comic intuitions, free verse and traditional strategies, dignity and slang, high song and plain speech, epigrammatic turns and warmer moments. And why not? A book of poems is not a philosophical tract, where the writer, having thought his way past pits and boulders, reaches at last a level assurance, expressed as a matter of course in a single tone of voice. A book of poems is allowed to mark the pits and boulders; it is even allowed to mark nothing else and never reach any destination at all. I am perfectly content, therefore, to have each poem be, in Wallace Stevens' wonderful phrase, the "cry of its occasion", and to have it deliver (if the fates are willing) its separate little shock of pleasure as if the others did not even exist. Poems are not improved by being consistent with others.

To make pleasure a trifle easier, I have jotted down a note here and there, and tried not to be officious. As for the "learned allusions" which I have left to speak for themselves, they are so lightly learned that they will not trouble a child in the vicinity of a *Columbia Encyclopedia*.

Finally, let me name and thank the journals in which poems of mine have appeared over the years:

Georgia Review	*Prairie Schooner*
Epoch	*College English*
Western Humanities Review	*Accent*
San Francisco Review	*Northwest Review*
Mutiny	*Southwest Review*
The Literary Review	*Hudson Review*

The poem entitled "We Who Do Not Grieve in Silence"

was commissioned by E. A. Glikes and F. Schwaber for their volume *Of Poetry and Power: Poems occasioned by the presidency and by the death of John F. Kennedy* (New York, Basic Books, 1964). It too has been revised for this collection.

Localities

AT THE "NUMBER SIX", CHELSEA
1956

Disinherited but dignified,
alone to the right, the same to the left,
I sip my profound espresso
this tolerable night.

Thirty rolls of the sun, with each
another east and west and in between,
sipping any nation, forced to be
the gentleman you cannot reach.

This sterling English I bagged like a thief,
dropping, so greedy was I, of Vienna,
Cracow, Flanders and Gaul good coin
as I ran: sure I must come to grief.

Yet most were kind. Some offered me
a chair. Few blamed the absence of a face.
What saved my happiness, in sum,
was middling courtesy.

Content, I leave a middling tip and rise.
My home is any fragrant history.
When stones have failed, and beams are scarce,
a tent, Vitruvius, must suffice.

THE FOUNTAIN OF TREVI

"Enzo!"

　　"Fabrizio!"

　　　"Cafone!"

A brat wades into the basin to retrieve the coins,
　　sopping shoes, pants and shirt, immemorial and
　　clutchy.

Mothers and fathers and mothers and fathers are
　　bawling out their slippery kids or wetting them
　　with juicy-lipped kisses.

And now a fresh damp load of heated tourists. The
　　cameras salute the statues.

Boys ogle ogled girls. Somebody is selling pictures
　　of exactly what we're all looking at.

The Fiats and Lambrettas fart into the hubbub, the
　　walls and shops of the piazza echo the smelly
　　sputter, our lungs turn black.

Legs dangle as we sit tier on tier; my feet in their
　　sandals ache like African troopers.

The bearded generation in undershirts and tatters
　　glower or sleep artistically or munch a crust; the
　　girls look as if their thoughts if any are fatal.

Suddenly a Midwesterner has offered a horse-and-
　　buggy man three thousand, who insists like a
　　record on five, he doesn't work winters, the

polyester wife is miserably embarrassed, they
get off, I can't see who won, the bald head
sweats with anger, the horse clobbers off.

We're bushed. A small policeman launches a
monstrous quarrel with five men, they're having
a grand time, like movie Italians, the kids are
yelping to help the quarrel along.

Two foreigners are gazing, wonderstruck, at the
Fountain,

At the imperious god

The pointed finger

The Triton storming the steeds, the uprushing
outrushing steeds, the imagined clamor of the
conch,

Noble the cascade, the swung stone noble.

Somebody is adding figures on a pad, the day's
expenses, and picking his nose with the pencil's
tiny eraser. His eyes bob from the figures to
the figures.

Close to the rim, a foliage of Japanese takes root
for a minute in "a glory of the West". Their
smiles rustle, unfading, among their private
syllables.

"Fabrizio, vieni quà, subito!"

Two shrivelled local old ladies have come out for the
cool air, the horses are so deep in their viscera
they will be found only at the hour of the

supreme recapitulation, neighing.

What to do, oh flesh, with the stone's reproof, "Be
beautiful, you, you, behave with musical rigor,
manifest even at lunch a palatine demeanor."

What to do? My feet smell. But we are here, are we
not, here, not over there admiring the city
dump.

And the water is clean, not even the kids throw peels
and wrappers in it,

And maybe not simply because the little cop is there;
who's afraid of him anyway? his quarrel
swallows him up, you could walk away with Mr.
Neptune.

This congregation I call a beginning, the beginning
that has been beginning since the beginning,

You marvels, you immortal impossible water and
marble demand.

Notes. Cafone: a boor, a lout. Vieni quà, subito: come over here
at once.

BREAKFAST AND JUKEBOX ON PIAZZA TRASIMENO

Carabinieri on this August morning
when it does me good to see the sun
in its blue dish — although you guard
(keeping an eye on pretty girls and for the rest
making a slouch of it) — although you guard
the Soviet Mission come to sell who knows
what toothsome derricks for Catania
(they hatch their commerce in the sweetest oleandered
loggiaed vined and pined palazzo
walls have ever kept from thieves like me),
you will not, will you, keep my Adriana
and myself from dancing one long tango in the street,
to mark (if nothing else) the anniversary of now,
for it was now last year today, and then
last April it was now, and Caesar too
was now, for Caesar did not live in Caesar's past
nor can a clock however sluggish fall behind.

Soldiers! I swear we plot to throw no bomb.
Who would throw bombs except at funerals?
The tango turns us to and fro, they stare at us
my lovely dear, they wonder as we fool about,
If, say, we caught a Russian head among these pines,
might we not plant a kiss under its hat?
Are they to act in case of sudden bliss?

PERSPECTIVES

1

Place a cottage
in these dolomites.
In this abominable beauty
place, brother,
a brotherly light.

2

Ice: elbow
between these cottages.
Push, colossals,
from too much brother
too much brother.

ROBBERS

In Naples a gang of experts
cracked our car in the glass eye
we were lunching standing up a block away
and they knew it
scootered off with my suitcase
leaving a dabble of blood.

The fat women were all over us
we were thumped and yanked with advice good advice
no one had seen a thing.

Now thinking of them standing that suitcase
on a dinky table and counting out my underwear
Adrienne's pearls my nice plans for another farce
my blue blazer and the rest, I see these articles
looking around flabbergasted at being pawed
by queer foreigners obviously no friends of the family.

"Where's daddy?" cries my property
spitting mad and scared to death.

Lousy gangsters,
are they laughing their heads off around that table?
No, this is business, they're serious,
one of them has a date
to go dancing tonight, Mamma is waiting
home with dinner for the two others,
they're in a hurry
and laughing their heads off.

Listen, children, listen jacket, sweater old friend,
        suits, shoes, pearls,
maybe there's hope, the blood, let's not forget
the good brown blood above the chrome

you couldn't see because you were inside the suitcase

Hey hey one of the bastards may be in (pray God)
for sensational convulsions witnessed by fainting nurses
maybe he'll die corroded blue and green
from messing with my underwear.

Yes but where's the satisfaction
where's the bliss
if I don't see it blue and green
with my own two eyes
or read it on page seven under local news?

If they all wind up in a Ferrari
I'm done with this damned galaxy.

COL DU GRAND SAINT BERNARD

Glaciers heels up heads down
drivel Rhône or slaver Pô.
From what icy imbeciles
these grandeurs flow!

ELEVEN FIFTY-NINE

Two cows are galloping in Normandy.
Slowly a moment forms, and God stands still.
A worm millimeters on a stone.
The road, fondling a tractor in its lap,
Inhales in Normandy. A rooster soloes.
A wall loses a sliver. Nothing dies.

Noon noon, cry the churchbells, noon noon.

                                        God moves.

A wasp and I exchange an ugly look.

                    —*Cerisy-la-Salle, July 27, 1978*

THE RADICAL VISITS LA BAULE

Let her enjoy her crème de menthe while she has it,
    The rich old biddy
    On the terrace at La Baule

Varnished, niftied, poodled, girdled, jewelled —
    Cripes it's like seeing
    A tombstone crack a smile.

Make no mistake, her cops'll bite your head off
    If they catch you tying your shoelace
    Against her U.S. Cadillac.

When she was born and let her first squawk out
    They underpaid five females to go
    Goo goo goo and look like they meant it.

And when she buys a hanky she gets chauffeured to it
    And a six-foot goon
    Trundles it out for her.

Go on, drink up, but wait we'll blast the opals off your
    fingers,
        We'll make you eat your Louis Fifteen,
        You'll scrub latrines down on your knees.

And never mind who'll wear the bloody opals next.

Note. La Baule, seaside resort in Brittany.

FIDEL CASTRO ASSUMES POWER

Out in Cuba the bold new shovellers dig and hoe.
Here in New York fascinating Europeans know.
    Mankind, we see, must always choose:
    There are two devils, and two dues.

—*1960*

CAMP GORDON 1953

In recollection of the time of the hot hospital
down in Georgia in the United States
with pneumonia caught inhaling murder
and drilling with the jolly men
God had blasphemed against the earth:
                    they paid him back the same.

First sick-call
where they believed my fever
and authenticated the fainting I had done
with such dark paradise of soul that day
marching to the tom-tom of the sun, the cannibal.
Second the trouble with the human item at the desk
who asked me "your religion bud?"
to fill a certain blank in case of death
and shivering I said None, before God none,
none by God, Goddamit none,
until they found a bed for me in a ward
full of his youngsters, black and pink,
the ones he jettisoned all over earth:
                    they paid him back the same.

That was a sweet pneumonia
although my orders were I must survive.
I did not eat the pills,
I rubbed thermometers, I groaned,
but slowly I recovered, I began to hear
the seven radios of the ward:
one ad, one negro southern spiritual howl,
one hit, one ad, one jazz, one news,
one quiz of decent ladies
all together in my bed,
whatever God had bellowed to the earth:
                    they paid him back the same.

At night I went in slippers and pajamas
to a patch of grass
behind a door I shut.
I walked criss-cross and in a circle,
hearing honest insects chirp,
and while I walked, I sang against my time
untimed cantatas in remembered scraps.
I sang like a demented naked man
the cops haul off the street
while all the damsels laugh to see his skin.
Then I returned to bed, the lights went out,
and no one knew
I had then overthrown our consecrated State,
the duly constituted government of man.
Now I slept, awaiting orders,
between a private and a corporal
great God had fumed against the earth:
                    they paid him back the same.

RAINY SEASON IN BARRACKS

On Sunday all the rain fell down.
We cursed. Then Fuji disappeared,
Although he stood so close, blue days
We soldiers did our duty on his gown.

The roofs were drumming, midnight fell at six,
The grass swam in a soup of mud.
We gargled air and used wet hands
To squeeze the water from our cheeks.

On Sunday Shunkwan smiled and gave a wink.
He said, "So heaven wills." One could not walk,
One could not pay nephews a call
Or plant a shrub, but one could think.

We cursed some more, next boredom made us ill,
But then we drank such Yankee gin
That all the walls came down. And Shunkwan said,
"Each man improves according to his skill."

—Camp Fuji, 1954

TO OVID, FROM ARMY BARRACKS

Rome drove you from the middle of a repartee
far from the Forum and the late levees,
beyond the unctuous slaves, the wicked plays,
to growl, they hoped, with Scythians of the gross black
    sea.
There you continued laughably to pare your nails
(while all your neighbors tore their meat with theirs);
you cited Virgil, kept some small parterres,
slept early. Hags in the woods boiled skins and scales.
Clutching your mother past, you took your pen again,
and weeping toward Caesar on his hill,
the song was Rome, the art was Roman still:
the syllables kept order in their pain.

A CHILD AT THE SEASIDE.

Her mother prods her
And what can she do?
She lunges, laughs, waddles back, cries, attacks again,
    babbles at the spray,
Fumbles, in short, for the human civilized attitude to
    the sea.
The Mediterranean kittens with her shins and submits.
The mother, centuries old, smiles, and, smiling,
Grows the child.

Somewhere, the fates are teaching
A newborn ant how to carry a speck.

Lying in the sand, inexhaustible,
I blink for the hundred forty millionth time.

MANY MANY

A moppet asks:
"How many sand is there in the whole wide world?"
I answer:
"Fifty-seven dillion grillion killion."

Because I do not care.
It's only when I think of ants or us:
Then I begin to sweat.
Back, child, back to sand.

THE DESERTED BEACH

When my spare time began I stretched under the gulls
Morning till evening slightly beyond the murder of the
    waves
Where the beach was soft to sift and I thought little
Of little, dun, like flotsam, nowhere bloomed anything
With remotely a soul, and the sea before me caused and
    sang
Such indiscriminate verbs, at evening
Troubled I went home troubled to the husband and the
    wife
Under a lamp, words and we huddled together,
But there we are, space the round ghost utters his look.

When it rained over my holiday, the window
Did not leave the corner of my eye, the seaweed's
    solitude
In the rain besieged me, and I thought the wasted noise
Of all that ocean looking for its ear, while the gray tree
Dodged, and lifted hands, and sidled, and could not
    parry
The father rain, yet grows indifferent to the whip.
I thought too the stuttering waves I almost deciphered,
And repeated the stinging sand yesterday under my
    feet.

And I returned in the sun from morning till evening
As my vacation continued, and the sand mistook me
For its people, as the sea met the seagull and the sky
Held the sun to his breast. The subtle sand-flies
Walked over my breast, finally I grew up wood, flies
Crawl as meteors do, hush, oh now the sea struck up
Gull and me and wood, and I obtained in moral
    darkness
Egregious patience. At last I am less than a man.

I stayed to let the legged stars cross me like insects
And while the moon was cawing and the gulls rotated
While my bones ebbed in the influence of clouds, I won,
Home I shall go like sand blown to the door immune.

THE CONCEPTIONS OF THE INTELLECT

Fool of a Freudian,
what if God had made it His provision
we should light upon him (glory glory)
through the bearded figure of a mortal dad?

Fool of a Christian
to believe it might be so.

Three o'clock: on the lake
the sun places a flock of suns,
which a placid wind erases
at three o'clock and three.

THE CLOCK IN THE FLEA MARKET
(Amsterdam)

(I'll call it he, may I?) He'd come on wicked times
and hadn't tried to set them right long ages long,
he couldn't tick, he'd lost his chimes,
the key was gone, and now they'd made him sit among
disgraceful skirts, cracked tables and a perishing rug —
so bad four Dutchmen grinned when I
(small hero) asked to pick him up,
and "will it work?" I risked, and "well I'll try."

He wasn't what the Spanish Court would offer Louis
or cunning Louis bestow upon a dainty Pope,
no dolphins in his hair, no naiad on his knee,
no amethysts or silver Faith and Hope;
plain wood he stood, plain honest face,
Dutch homely square
and solid anabaptist grace,
one flower carved into his chest with modest care;
but he had lived with lace
and stood proud, stiff and mute against the slum.

I gave my seven guilders, found a key,
affixed a vagrant pendulum,
turned nuts and screws, and set him free.
With feeble health and anxious grain he sat
and pressed a cushion in my car
to make and to survive the journey to my flat.
The city was not plush: a street gave us a jar,
then twenty more; came cobblestones and tramway
    rails
and turns to take and brakes to squeeze and stops to
    make —
they poked him into life with clucks and wails
and whirrs, a wooden ache,

a knocking rib, slim gongs
of fright and bells of trouble,
in short, a hospital of wrongs.
But when at home I saw him upright in his rubble
and looking like a magistrate
whose air ascribes his belch to creaking furniture,
I undertook — and swore upon his horizontal pate —
come blossom or come burr,
come landlord, wife or maid,
to hoist him up on any shelf I'd ever own,
dusted, warmed and wound, and tenderly displayed.

I've kept my word. The years dropped in, went home.
The hours migrated chime by chime.
Sometimes I heard, and often not, his mild
and just and confidential sign
the span is rotting under me and like a child
I must fall down, there is no hold.
He's grown a touch more grim this year (his age I
    guess).
No matter: I prefer the sentence told
his way; his dialect alarms me less.

EMPTY HOUSE

In the middle of a house
a clock strikes one
(strikes one?)
to no one.

Vibrations lunge
(who knows)
at chairs and sleeping
bibelots.

Why does the world
bother to be
without me?

At two,
a shift of dust
proves a vibration
was and must.

Or did it shift
to rendez-vous
with my two eyes
at two?

Why does the world
bother to be
without me?

Stars fiddling
ten billion years,
and not even
a pair of ears?

SLANTED BIRD

The unleafed branches of the tree in March
radiate, inverted parasol,
serious and quasi analytical.

That is when Nature plays the clown,
comes in and daubs a slanted bird
across a twig,

tousles the organization:
a whistle at a discipline,
a comma at the clause's end,

ONE OF THE ASTRONAUTS ATE A PIECE OF CONSECRATED BREAD ON THE MOON

The Reverend blessed a slice of bread,
   Aldrin took it to the moon,
To prove man is and shall remain
   Half sage, two-thirds buffoon.

—1969

FATIGUE

If there is heaven it must be
simplicity,
where nuns do secretively go
with heavy-hearted lads and girls;
they dance with saddened chemists
and they kiss
the desperado atheists.
Where every cross becomes a parallel
timelessness may make us well,
and prove
profundity a spoof,
problems mistaken, and complication Hell.

PRAYER

Time lays out good times like beads upon a string,
A kiss, a thought, a music and a Spring.

Paradise be simultaneous everything,
Eternity obviate remembering.

Two Flakes of Joy

INTROIT

Forgive me, you so pitifully dead,
The dance which young I danced and yet return to
    dance,
As I forgive — reluctant — in advance —
Swingers on my grave, tumblers in my bed.

—1977

COME PLAY

The twenty-sixth of April warm needles
Are reported in the air.
Our sun blooms elegant. In areas of noon
Young suicidal men who dwelled all winter
On a ragged incunabulum
Have come in danger of a dancing foot.
Consider, Liz! an inkling of the wind
Speeds all the leaflets to each others' arms,
A touch of Spring suasion
Puts the candles to their prayers
In the first-come chestnut tree,
Azaleas set themselves on fire,
And the cocked eye of the sun
Stirs every crocus from his pillow.
Oh Liz, why should two lovers shuffle
Who could, if they'd but half agree,
Ignite the scene perenially?

FALLING

Love is simple
Inevitability.
Drop a pebble
From a tree.
If there's no choice
But earth for it,
That pebble's me.

FEVER

The man you choose to love
should disbelieve in rain
run mad on Mondays
tickle generals under the stubbled chin
and never die.

I myself am nearly come to this,
because you threw me, absent-mindedly,
one entire courteous word.

SONG

Today April today
the new grass jungles
and the green birds play.

While sun plods
up a higher noon
on ladder clouds

a high-strung
wind concealing
his sentimental lung

grumbles
where a bud babies
and fumbles

and terrifies
a newborn moth
with jests of ice.

This week April this week
Eros flies in,
the world turns Greek.

My young eye swarms
where open girls
bare dangerous arms.

Before tongues dare,
decisions dart,
we flirt mid-air.

We have no name,
we never met,

but all the same

we prophecy
the kiss the quarrel
the promise the lie

and mean "shall we?"
as flower bends
to flowering bee,

as moon slips out
her grasping
corpulent cloud,

and ocean lifts
his waves where she
soever drifts.

GOSPEL

It's sienna all the way,
It's lady-slippers, grass deliriums.
No bookish God is peeping
With a scimitar inside his fist
These seconds Greek with liberty.
So let's abuse a clover bed
And pull the wind about us
Like a coverlet. Oh splendid news,
One hundred horses drive the sun,
Young Pan hauls Methodists away,
And flights of nuns are caught
In zigzags of vociferous bees . . . .

AGAINST PRUDENCE

Some death fetches
like a brisk police
that collars innocents at drink
or lovers at their kiss.

But cowards run
to their own tomb
(a funeral of one
into his own cocoon).

As though they couldn't wait,
they dig a solid hole
and sneak under a cross
to smother their own soul.

My love is one of such.
I say that she must break
her dolls and idols, burn
a city for my sake,

Cross husband, mother, god,
fool inconvenient laws,
love passion and rank honesty
and loathe peculiarly remorse.

And she, not answering, she only
loves me with a gaze,
like an incurable
who understands his case.

THE JAIL

sentenced to
the universe of me
let lips, let arms debar
the worse jail, liberty

you'd breathe
with a constricted chest
independent on
an Everest

since Adam
poor man went and sinned
kindly walls stand
to the cruel wind

LOVER'S MAXIM

The wounds of love bleed boiling red.
Prudence, dear, is colored dead.

WHEN NOBODY LOOKS

Elizabeth for long.
That is official
And in company:
A bow to the throng,
Handsome gentility.

Liz for short.
The sound's like the quip
Of a bee snatching
Honey for sport,
And buzzing her wing.

But *Lisa* is the time
Four hands whisper and do
In two bodies' nooks
Like children at their little crime
When nobody looks.

SONG

My love answers my love;
   into lips lips sink
and one same milk,
   each other, drink.

What are to me
   Chaos and Flood?
My love touches
   my only blood.

The cannon's concussion

finds us asleep
like harvesters blithe
   after the reap.

No newscast tells the world
   its chemistry is changed
and by two flakes of joy
   the cosmos rearranged.

Month buries our day,
   year raises the stone;
let rubbing wind
   make us unknown.

DR. WATSON TO DULCINEA

I gave my joy long kisses thigh to thigh
   December night, the solstice of our love,
   ascending toward the Christmas of the seed
   and feeding the poor universe with yet
another bone devoted to a bone.

For all we knew that love is fiber, tissue,
   cell leaping with intelligence of cell,
   we ranted ''soul'' we raved ''enchantment'':
   two compounds ionized into rebellion.
And yet the rebel's cry, albumin too . . . .

THE JOURNEY

For three days, good-bye,
and in this thimble of time
oceans of apprehension lie.

IMPATIENCE

Slow, oxen hours, witless muddy animals,
I sit astride you
Shoving you with my buttocks,
I shout at you with the sweat in my face or
Beg you beg you to get forward with my best furious
  cajoleries
And then again give you a knock between your ears
  with my fist,
But nothing.
You take your insolent time, of course.
I have to rejoice
You lift those paws of yours at all
And now and then we leave a tree behind.

A LILY AND A CHUNK OF COAL

The gods too hate to work.
Believe me though, it was not craziness that moved
   them
when they wrenched our two antipodes
               I think of muscle-men in circuses
               twisting metal pipes
to make us meet: was ever passion
farther-fetched than ours? Yet

''Not the conquest of Peru
not the Trans-Siberian Railway
and not the inquisition of old Saturn
matter more''
they said
and forced our iron longitudes.

Honey gods, lovelies of heaven,
you never were less crazy . . .

THE GARDEN

I place you in a garden
but a garden twenty times
as good as paradise,
with hordes of flowers
and grass marching in legions
where a toadstool would get lost
if a toadstool could be found
disgracing in my garden
twenty times
as good
as paradise.

And over you an orange sun
contracted for eleven in the morning
in incessant May,
a cloud or two
for humor and trees
trees making a great windy rush
to stay precisely where they are,
near you of course,
spying out of every green and rascal leaf.

And round about
I stick a wide and nasty wall
made of the foulest foul brown stone
which looks as if it always rained on it,
besides electric wires, spikes,
and here and there a hungry dog.
As I can't fly
I add a stingy gate
locked by a ton of steel
to which the only key is in my pocket.
The gate is smart and understands
I am the janitor and king.

The rest? I'll eat my tongue.
When it is I come,
and how it is you greet me,
the weight and contour of our dialogues,
the kiss that interferes
with topics of importance,
the bodies in their moist entanglements,
you know, I know,
we spread no gospels —
although that daisy
standing by our keel its yellow eye wide open
that daisy I suspect
is learning dimly in its roots
there's more to nature than the bureaucrats of pollen
and the sniff of lowly snouts.

PLENITUDE

I sing under my beard
a basso folderol of note.
The fly cancels no promenade,
I jostle neither sun nor mote.

I sing the crazy mood a leper has
come back new-fangled to the street.
The windows do not rattle,
I hear the rain's soft centipede.

And holstering his pistol
by my door, the regular gendarme
retrieves his ear, calls off his eyes,
reports the situation calm.

NO MORE POEMS

While I loved unwinningly
I told the public. Poetry!
Now, desiring nothing more,
I padlock lips and door.

UNSAFE I REPLY

Lovers, like emperors
of crumbling Rome,
sway proudest and strongest
the first day of throne.

Their stride and their spring
is such as gave men
the heavenly notion
of man before sin.

Limber with worship,
calm after lust,
they smile at a crumb
and are happy with dust.

What follows we know:
spies in the cellars,
rumors, familiar remarks
of fortune-tellers,

an old, lyrical rose
in a gully,

tantrums of fear,
and then the last folly,

not to depart
but sullenly sit
clutching scepters and rings
which no longer fit.

To this, says divination,
we must come as well:
Love is a nomad,
duration his hell.

He comes like a storm
uprooting the trees;
He goes like the hem
of a tattered breeze.

Unsafe I reply:
be small with me.
Let's huddle unsafe
beneath history,

and plot to continue
affectionate fools
not worth the notice
of maxims and rules.

DECLINE AND FALL

What shall I see in this extinguished light?
A dogwood blooming in December?
A banker sobbing on his typist
for the sin of being rich?
Spider with his rueful legs giving
flies their liberty? Hare calling
her hunter? Ribald saint? Buddha in a pet?
Or, my love, continuance of love,
decanted once with such a dipping
of the heart, I thought I'd drunk of it,
poor me, a passing immortality?

REPINE, REPINE

If it is ill to be an underground
And dry he-was, it is much worse to room
By arctic cliffs where seals are shivering
And sunlight rarely interlopes, and know
You dance meantime inside the circle
Of heartwhole fat peonies. Death is not cruel
Since we're all lost; it's caste I hate: to be
The varlet while a princess plies her minuet.

THE ART OF REMEDIES

Let me wholly put my mind
To Caracalla's hunted Rome,
To Albigensians burning
Pimple, hair, and toe,
To Asia rationing a rind.

Humane lament will tell
My own, perhaps, to blush,
For though I sulk and bite my lip,
My grief is not on earth's
Noteworthy parallel.

WOUNDED PHILOSOPHER

They note that I am glum. I tell them why.
Crime is not crime. Love is self-tickle. The sun
    petrifies.
Try is cracked. God dissolved. Undamned I die.

Are these not cause enough? They nod, impressed, I
    see.
Nitwits. My woman left. I cry.

Explanatory note

Shall ontologic pain be more
Than (say) my thumb caught in the door?

THE WISE AND THE GOOD WILL NOT FOOL ME

The wise and the good will not fool me,
my own language it's the tough language of sense:
I haven't got one me for books and dress
and one to use on muddy Tuesdays.

Not that I never heard of selfless love,
immortality, free choice, our duty,
and the unique consciousness of mankind;
who hasn't heard rave the wise and the good?

Come, woman, undress, your husband's away,
your children snore, space is bent with pain.
Root your fingers in the soil I am.
I will leave you at the first noble word.

THE EGG THE MOTHER THREW

The egg the Mother threw
that burst in Zeus and Christ and man,
in Egypt and in Babylon,
has hatched (don't giggle) me and you,

To raise this bedtime doubt:
was that conflagration fixed
to kindle two such silly sticks,
are we what bibles shout about?

Go wash, and pin your hair,
and let us, while I knot my tie,
submit that in our Mother's eye
we are, like Christ and cabbage, there.

OLD MAN IN LOVE

Never envy the young.
They are rivers
that cannot flow without flooding,
they are magnates
who give to wrong charities,
and they fall with lamentable wounds
over a straw in an alley.

We are different.
We are as different as the hunter
with a last bullet,
and the ice of his great hunger.

SULLEN MYRMIDONS POISON THE WEEDS

Sullen myrmidons poison the weeds
Lest an enemy survive.

In a ruin two lovers huddle.
A booted lout guffaws.

In his low brain one atom shifts.
We must love on.

The Wind Must Brutalize My Dust

I AM A LITTLE SNAIL

I am a little snail
On the green grass I sail
Sometimes I live sometimes I die
And in between I hear great mankind cry
We mankind must survive
How ghastly to deprive
The cosmos of mankind
Although the reason I don't find
Being a simple snail
On the green grass I sail

WORDS FOR JOHN STRACHEY'S
ON THE PREVENTION OF WAR

John Strachey was his simple name.
In Britain flew his middling fame.

He thought of war. His manly spirit shook.
To kill off war he wrote a book.

The H-bomb would exterminate us all.
Therefore (he reasoned) let it never fall.

John Strachey hoped that realistic negotiation
Would avert unthinkable obliteration.

We shall (he wrote) survive, if we agree
Upon a Super-Power World Authority.

Already he detected "a new attitude of mind."

With this the book came out and the reviews were kind.

But then he died. John Strachey, looking forward,
     died.
No H-bomb struck him, just the regular foul scythe.

John Strachey, after all, one truth forgot:
Man may survive, but men do not.

—1964

Note. John Strachey, author, Labour MP, and secretary for war
     from 1950 to 1951.

DO NOT PLACE YOUR TRUST IN BABIES

Do not place your trust in babies:
Himmler was one.
Remember he too took his first steps
on funny pudgy legs,
you should have seen him gurgle
and smile at the smiles he saw.
Ah what a happy family.

Next time you bend over a cradle
tuck a hatchet in your thoughts.

THE ADVANTAGE OF TRIVIA

Clever I have made a circle
and inside I stir my tea, ambition,
ladies, votes, and poetry,
and all my paltry erudition.

I keep as busy with my clutter
as a baby with his blocks,
I keep as busy as one
of all the yapping hunting dogs.

Keep busy is the rule of men
too shrewd to be too wise.
There is no horror in the air
but where we realize.

ME FOR SOFT FLOORS AND SMARTLY NOT
TO THINK

Me for soft floors and smartly not to think.
Vase at the window, carpet, couch, no books.
Smart in the wind a lamppost tickled
by a tree gives me a yellow, measurable wink.

I loathe the moon, and do the beauty and the stars.
Me keep me far from distance. They utter
my how dim I am how dumb I talk,
they light me naked up this mammal farce.

How can those nitwit lovers bear the sky?
me for a chandelier hung not too high.

FRAGMENT

Stay with me
and say no solemn word before the dog howls
and I die. Play me over and again
the rhythm and the render of a leaf
and do not say the wind must brutalize
my dust. Oh friskers, ruffians,
forgetters and unknowers,
I am no Jeremiah
eyeing horribly amused Jerusalem.
I dream a man at sixty may yet curl
his tongue about the berry he has plucked.
I hear the balloting for spruce or fir
among the nationalities of birds . . . .

TO MY COUSIN STELLA
(d. 1944)

I am walking, fed and tranquil, with a book.
Near a broken wall
a girl lies on the ground.
Her dead hand holds a dead grenade.
Half her face torn out and both her eyes dead open
like two bulbs gone out.

She says: "Is this the Ledger of Our Blood?"
And I: "It is the book of Aucassin and Nicolette,
a mild small book
of decent merriment
and songs between
like poppies in a field."

She says: "Machine guns made me what I am,
machine guns smote me running in the field."

I kiss the crust of blood
but the lady spoke saying
Here is Nicolette your dearest
who has returned from distant lands to

"Howl the world sick
womb howl hand howl
breast gut throat howl howl"

And nothing else,
save, shock on shock, farther than I cry to see,
a shameless wheat pushing against the crow.

THE HOMBURG-HATTED MAN

Going my corrugated way
I stop two laughing pealing veering
sun-outsunning children about eight.
"You two!" "Yes sir?" (a little downed)
"Five years and then a gavel
chinks the simple cup the boy has been
and crack you will be men."
They stare, dumb they gauge
the funny danger of the homburg-hatted man,
then crack indeed they gallop into space,
at fifty yards the cup chimes double loud forgetful
crystal holy hale.

FROM CHIHUAHUA TO THE BORDER

What they do out there, the mountains, is stand
stark useless; bleach (but why?) glued to the sun;
not one green hair grows on these rumps nor is heard
one woosh of a wing or grumble of a throat.
The road's a slap at them they don't know how to feel.
They wall us up (driving north) on either side of one
brown prostrate earth, we give them blank for blank,
until oh God who was it winked at them?
You, you, behind my yawn, you femurs,
ribcage, mandibles, sworn friends to me, you
plotting with foreigners, assassins in my house!

No, no, we love you, chime the bones; drive on, drive on.

VISCERA

After running five minutes
I lie on the grass and listen to my heart.

Sometimes I feel like calling down
the well of my body
"Organs, organs! Do you hear me? Discipline!"

Lord, to be dependent on a pancreas!

If it turns off I'm dead.
Do I choose to die? Not much!
Yet this fat machinery dares run me.

Salivating with indignation

I demand to be pure spirit,
I want to boss these lungs, these kidneys, this trash.

Did you, Plato, yes or no call them my slaves?
Then why does that slave keep thumping
When I shout "At ease"?

DITTY ON THE BRAVE MAN'S LOT

Wilfred Owen died in the World War
the darling of his rifle corps.
He volunteered, the way a great man ought,
and can't complain that he was shot.

I squinted, said I could not see;
the doctors paused; got rid of me.
I hate my land, hate mankind more,
and plan to live to ninety-four.

THE DESERTER'S DITTY

Alcaeus, Horace and Anacreon,
good cowards all (though brave in song):
I too grew nervous, dropped my gun,
and voted medals for the strong.

I favored too the bubbling of a kiss
above the tantrums of a bomb;
I did my duty to my private bliss,
Alcaeus, Horace and Anacreon.

Note. These three lyric poets all fled in battle, in deference to
the father of poets and cowards, Archilochus, who dropped
his shield and ran seven centuries before Christ when the
fighting got too hot. Alcaeus ran from the Athenians,
Horace ran at the Battle of Philippi, and Anacreon ran
from Cyrus the Great.

OPEN LETTER TO GOD

Sir, I've been looking up statistics.
Each 8 seconds a baby's born, each 20
1 wretch is removed. Tick tock it goes.
I find, considering this exercise
In conclusionless logistics,

The come-and-go is useless. For, you see,
Life always wins, but death never loses.
Since we (next point) are quite as good
As Babylon or Futurama, stop birth, stop death,
And stick with us: it's good sense, it's even charity.

I add, being old, I think each day better
Of your creation, and shall be glad
To settle for good on your ground floor.

Thank you, sir, for your attention to this letter.

BERCEUSE

The prisoner falls down a ditch
and clutching at his pain he sighs
"I'll stop a bit." A soldier shoots,
the prisoner tips over, dies.

The soldier jumps into a hole,
an airplane sees him where he lies.
The bullets make a dotty line,
the soldier bleeds a pint and dies.

Home goes the pilot up the wind,
alas a shell bursts as he flies.
He thinks of mother and himself,
dives into the ground and dies.

Beside his head a daisy stands,
the night spreads out the stars;
a blade of weed leaps round her stem,
the daisy chokes, death is no farce.

I rise and strut and din at God
"Pity! Comfort! And denounce!"
God says, "I note your claim," and winks,
and all the stars, applauding, bounce.

CONVERSATION WITH A TREE

Somewhere I don't know where,
what kind, maybe in Minnesota
where I may have been who knows,
there is a tree. "Good morning, dear,"
I say, "will it be really you,
you who sift the wind this province here
and whistle at your birds oh well?"
"Yes me; and is it really you,
with just two arms and still alive,
you with lips, you with eyes and legs
and whistling down to death oh well?"

There we met, we two, with great fine talk
of chance and how the atoms meet
with so much reason and no rhyme,
and how though strangers now, we must
be staying longer in each others' arms
than me with Joan or him with Jay.

And then I went my whistling way:
I have my shady nest by heart.

A YES FLY AND A NO FLY FOR JUDITH

one fly that came
one fly that went,
useless, random,
and content.

•

I do not wish
I were a fly;
I want to hate it
when I die.

MARCHING SONG

The dapper days are over,
   the dying must begin.
I was a crooked lover
   (nice song and mandolin)
but, customer of clover,
   I've reached the classic inn:
wooden mattress, wooden cover
   on a rotten skin.
If only I could savor
   one last girl's first sin!
Then damn and die the rover:
   Eternity, you win.

MIRACLE PLAY

Doctor

I'll speak straight out (you are a man).
   We'll pamper you two months or three,
but then — that nugget on your brain —
   yes, yes, it is a tragedy.

Patient

I have a wife, I have a child,
   I have a car, I have a lease,
I have a yard, I have a job,
   I have such love for all that is.

Angels that night

Our wings will tell you who we are,
   our wands will tell you what we can:
we are the sprites that gratify
   the last desire of dying man.

Patient

Please kill my wife, please kill my child,
   so I won't miss it, kill the world.
How dare these bodies play when oh
   under the floor my bones lie curled?

Jesting angels

We promise you, there is no world:
   that beauty which you see, you made,

and those that play, we swear, shall be
   invisibly by you unplayed.

God

For each man's death kills all the world,
   and each man takes the world to bed.
I am the kindest God of all,
   the clay I kill does not regret.

MEMORIAL DAY

When you bring flowers to my grave
it won't occur to you, needless to say,
how degrading it is to be dead —
forced to accept "a loving tribute"
from my betters, you, mournful, erect.
You'll think, no doubt, "how grateful he would be
if he could speak," and Christ I retch
thinking of me down there mouth shut and mousy meek
six feet under a stupid violet.

TO MY FATHER

Anxious to blame, I lift the past.
Let there be worms under the stone.

Like:
When I cried with exhaustion
you slapped me for crying.

Like:
I wished to be a poet. You,
predictable dealer, fumed.

Like:
When they put me in uniform,
you said: "It will make a man of you."

Like:
You blustered with the maids
but snivelled at the sight of any badge.

Like:
The week before you died
you took a fling at bankruptcy
hoping to defraud your creditors
six of whom were bosom friends.

Anxious to blame, I lift the past.
There are no worms under the stone.
I can't hate down my grief. It grows.
            Father!
Is it like you to hurt your child?

—1978

CHRISTMAS

I hear the ancient churchbells walk
and sow into the night
their charming seed, the God,
his courtesy, his might.

I hear them toll again again
in dulci iubilo!
May only we who slaughtered him
his black departure know.

WE WHO DO NOT GRIEVE IN SILENCE

1

First came the special issues of the magazines
With loyal photographs: the old rich times, the rocking
   chair,
The wife who knew who Dali is, the muscular war,
The politics retouched and smiling, the happy hammer
Of his power, the idiocy of death. Each fifty cents.

The president was dead, tears fell and incomes rose.
               Wait, brother, wait,
               My grief has gone to market too.

2

The picture books cost more but they were meant to last,
They used the most caressing words, like strong ideals
And dedicated heart and faith in our democracy.
And those who sold the plaster statuettes (one dollar
   each),
Their right hand mourned, their left rang up the cash.

The president was dead, laments and incomes rose.
               Wait, brothers, wait,
               My grief has gone to market too.

3

Congressmen deplored into the cameras, the voters saw
Their simple, manly sorrow. Foreign crowns were
   caught
Bowing usefully toward the poor man's grave.
All were shocked; what's more, they really were; alas
One could not keep one's honest sobs untelevized.
The president was dead, tears fell and reputations rose.
               Wait, brothers, wait,
               My grief has gone to market too.

4

Next came the records, and his voice was heard again
To make flesh creep from shore to shore. A publisher
Withdrew a luckless exposé; a sensitive biography
Recouped the loss. Three journalists retold the terror
Irreversible. We shuddered, covered up our eyes, and
   bought.

The president was dead, laments and incomes rose.
                             Wait, brothers, wait,
                             My grief has gone to market too.

5

When great men breathe their last, their expiration
Swells our sails. Films shall be turned, sermons
   released,
Memoirs composed and statues rooted. Pure grief is
   silent, true,
And yet pure hardness is too hard for us as well:
We are the double flip-flop flunkeys of the playing cards.

The president is dead; my poem goes to press.
                             Grief, brothers, grief
                             Is my profit, but all the same I
                                       grieve.

IAGO SHUT HIS MOUTH

Give him his due:
When Iago finished
His act,

Iago shut his mouth.
There was no chatter
In the man;

No urge
To start careers
After extinction.

EPITAPH

Life has been a little broom
And I have been a little dust.
Dust we know must leave the room,
For God we know is just.

And My Lids Fall Down

MOTION

A worm lifts up a somber eye
and sees how sweet it is to be a fly;
what gossips, raids, impressions, climates, fun!
he knows of flies that frolic in the sun.

The fly (you guess the tale) admires the worm,
enjoying on his decent inch the firm
tradition of a twig. His own head aches
with every sprint he undertakes.

Eagles beg of moles a fling at sod.
The truth is, God is bored with being God.
Why else did Zeus go slumming as a swan?
Why did the Verb go fooling as a man?

Cobalt minions shiver in the very stone.
And dissolution is the amusement of bone.

LIVING ROOM

I am haunted by eccentricity
and the opposite I am,
and afraid that underneath
my bearing so refined,
my presence unalarming,
underneath, indeed, my sane
responses to the wilderness,
my heart is perfectly inane.

One settee, two easy-chairs,

a low glass table and a walnut chest
stand on my almost Persian rug.
I own with modest pride the finest
false Chêng Tê money can buy.
Therefore I scratch my chin and say:
Shall I invite Medea, trailing blood,
up for cocktails after the play?

EASTER SUNDAY

In the tedium of my room all bulbs are lit
and stunned I attend to the walls
and sit.
I am mild as a sofa,
exact as a vase, rooted in carpets.
Christ blew the shofar
and I saw tonight the first green
pimples in a shivering tree
and I came home shocked to be seen
in company with life.
I am bored. I have had three experiences.
I want want. I am the antonym of knife.
Shall I learn gardening? Humus
under my fingernails might be amusing; I have heard
of snapdragons. Juvenes dum sumus.
At the outburst of the resurrection
a man must cross naked against the light
and pray softly in a vertical direction.
I am not morally fit to die.
I must as yet enact
what muscles imply.

Note. Juvenes dum sumus: While we are young, an old university
     song.

ENNUI

Oh Hannibal, I wish that I could ride an elephant,
and wipe my boot against an Alp.
I wish that I could suffer like a helmet
and eat crème glace at funerals.

But it is you, oh Hannibal, who plunge
out of the camps of edelweiss. You toss
the matrons of Campania to your chocolate boys.
Moustache erect, you call for poison, and you quaff.

Note. Crème glace: ice cream.

THE NINNY'S LAMENT

If you fair wind had blown me stronger,
    stranger than you did,
I would have been a crook, a matador,
    philanthropist, or wit.

But while I flew and flapped my wings,
    that secret wind went calm.
I dropped, I broke, my spring fell out,
    I do nor good nor harm.

Prince, who knows how great men bloom
    and we the ninnies rust?
Who knows what wind brings Hannibal,
    and what Augustulus?

Note. Augustulus, last of the Roman emperors, "an inoffensive
    youth" (Gibbon).

THE ECSTASY OF BROTHER GILES

And Saint Bonaventure replied very earnestly
with his usual authority
"Yes, the foolish old woman
is able to love God better than
the doctor, and is, indeed, in some sense
the very aim of our theology."

Then Brother Giles ran into the garden
and then to the gate, past three
holy admirable birds and the grass,
shouting and laughing many times between,
"Dumb silly peasant fool ho hey come here
she loves God better than our Bonaventure!"

And immediately fell into an ecstasy
which lasted hours on the petunias
in front of the sky while I sat up
in my beachchair amazed he felt no
inhibition before strangers, but tore his breast
open like a window and stuck his heart out
to heat it so directly in the sun
and cried and cried and was so happy.

Who bitter who invented facts?
nothing since has made me even sad.

THE PROOFREADER'S LAMENT

"Typewriters are amazing enemies
To lions and the crickets in a chirping head" —
These were the words young Jason said
When he hankered for a golden fleece

And dropped a dungeon overboard.
And Byron was a gaudy heart, a lout; in fine,
A baron with a nose for the sublime;
His day a color, and his night a sport.

Moreover, loonies there have been
Who climbed five flights into a leaking room
And therefore wove upon a loom
A sun, a zinnia, and a tangerine.

(A pencil on my thumb, I earn my keep,
Don't catch the moon, and look before I weep.)

CONCERNING BAUDELAIRE

Poor Charles he took his sins so seriously;
each time he bought a drink Man fell again;
he suffered himalayas; demons pinched him:
symbols oh yes, but still they smelled,

they had the good authentic gothic air
of meaning blood and giving hell
and swatting men between a woman's breasts.
Maybe he'd kissed his chère maman too much,

poor Charles, but come, it must have been quite nice

To feel that Lucifer himself broke through
Voltaire to damn you in particular
for poking at a Caribbean slut;

it must have been a treat to know a God
you could scare half to death by showing him
where two of his raw daughters mussed against
the code, "their ghastly cult unhinged the sun."

I envy you. I murdered several crowds
last war by soaking them in flames,
I hear the earth's about to burst, and what
I say is "well, well, well," and look about,

afraid I've overdone the fancy rhetoric.

THE SWIMMER WITH THE LONG CIGAR

There was a man who jumped because he felt like it into
    the sea
Off Florida (near Vero Beach) to swim he said to
    Tanezrouft.
They told him, those who knew, the place he named
    was far too far
And anyhow far in a continent far from the shore
And never had a drop of water dropped on Tanezrouft,
But "is that so?" said he and jumped into the sea
Off Florida, a cither in one hand and smoking a cigar;
The marvelous of which is that reporters saw him last
Doing the crawl between Bou Djebeha and Abelbodh
Although there never was a drop of water landed there
    as yet,

And he was chipper as a trout and had what's more
   acquired
The local dialect and two slave-girls who also swam.
But all I know about that man is that that was not me.

ON MY 29TH BIRTHDAY

Let's confer upon my elegy.
I'm twenty-nine, ah me, ah me.

Twenty-eight dear corpses, come near, come near,
I bring bad news for me to hear.

The price of glee is going up; please for a plan:
How shall I earn my chance to buy a little fun?

Twenty-seven, did you raise your metacarp?
Bone to bone, speak free, my sweet, and sharp.

"You're a bore." But is that all? "No. Go hoard
Each dime of luck that you can swindle or extort,

Save, be humble, watch your health, and fast:
At ninety-two you'll be the laugher who laughed last."

I'll be the laugher who laughed least.
"Then shoot yourself. Some fools are never pleased."

SUNDAY TWIDDLING THUMBS, PEEVISH AS A CHILD

I'm not fond of anyone
and no one's fond of me.
It's the devil of a joy,
I tell you, to be free!

Should they find me in a pool
of blood tomorrow on my bed,
they'd bury me like a tin can
the way I was, still wet.

My friends (I have a pack)
would say, "So much for wit,
and doing neither harm nor good,"
and talk two days of it.

Unless I give some chocolates
and retail a compliment,
to buy God willing half a sob
that will be really meant.

MAN IS WHAT ANIMAL

Chapter One
Man is the animal that laughs.

Chapter Two
Man is the only species warring on itself.

Chapter Three
Man is the religious animal.

Chapter Four
Man is the cosmos become conscious of itself.

Chapter Five
Have you seen how endlessly and mellow
A cat lies on his pillow?

What have you done with us, my Lord?
Man is the animal that's bored.

ENNUI IN NOVEMBER

Here me,
there the first flog of winter, smart at the street,
trees like the glow of a skin slapped, red with pain
but not warmth.
The leaves' umbilical
scissored by November from the mother
and harsh the wind diving under the window
to my skin.
I could wish:
me stupid with solitude and books and brain,
an ice to find me, a tiger, a December,
and I'd bleed.

ENNUI

A bird shins up a tree,
   the clocks run after time,
the Senate spits a law
   against eternal crime,

Fresh factories go wild.
   There's so much progress on,
Idleness itself snores louder,
   and my lids fall down.

Poems After

AFTER ROBINSON JEFFERS: *"Come peace or war, the progress of Europe and America becomes a long process of deterioration."*

What acreage has calamity
more than *I die*?
I died at maximum of Greece
before Protagoras disturbed its sky;
I died at England's best: Raleigh crossed the seas
but nothing was my destiny;
and in America's first dignity
and last, in spite of Jefferson's augustan eye,
I was obliged to die.
Let Europes and Americas abstractly rot.
Death occupies a smaller lot.

AFTER DANTE

My mind dwells perfectly on death's incommodation
and nothing safe. I hate noble literature
and professional wisdom: that famous Roman
calm at his blather before they broke him on the
    rack . . . .

The night I opened Hell and saw Ugolino set
his teeth into Ruggieri's head, I turned my own away,
but slow enough to catch Ruggieri's muddy grin,
and then the teeth struck bone and I was forced to look.

His hair bleeding (and Ugolino's upper lip
was pushed against his nose from biting) Ruggieri
    grinned,

Ruggieri said: "Yet I am I"; and I crouched stunned;
there is no cruelty to match no God at all.

Me for the rectangular bed and humus
my eternal coverlet, bone beneath pain,
not even crying, Someone drill a hole and thrust
a tube in mercy to periscope some sky to me . . . .

May my father and my mother die suddenly
and old, like lights switched off by accident, and not
be frightened. May I not dangle after my friends
alone to be shot like an only target in a square,

no one to hide behind and hope he will die first.
I am nervous and yet I would welcome a ghost.
I have lifted my mind, which is glory, but why?
To dwell on death without hole or consolation.

Note. That famous Roman: Boethius.

AFTER LI PO

In a gentle silent pond
A jade pavilion stands;
Close by its door, among the fronds,
A bridge bows to the land.

And in the chamber sit
Three friends who drink warm tea;
They chat, and now and then they twit,
They laugh each time they disagree.

And in the gentle pond

A fish jumps at a fly.
The fly must stomach the affront.
No choice, the thing must die.

So still, so polished is the pond,
The house and bridge peep upside down,
And upside down the friends so fond,
The figured cups, the silken gowns.

But right side up and nothing else
The fish jumps at the fly.
The story which this story tells
No roguish mirror turns awry.

AFTER WALLACE STEVENS: *"The imperfect is our
    paradise."*

I too, undoubtedly, I too
I should have ventured to conceive
this world as turquoise, aware
but softly of the streak which marred
its blue primordial. Not marred,
not so (I too, I should have said):
that darker but still blue distress
enriched the stone's peculiar price,
for blue naively blue, the lake
untampered by its island,
glib blue would make orfèvres yawn,
I too, aware, I should have said.

But could this be? I came too late.
And yet I tried. My fingers held
that delicately irritated stone,
exquisite with sin, until

the symbol failed. "Am I," a Jewess
twelve years old inquired softly
of her elders and her betters,
"the discord that beguiles the song?"

She was the flimsiest among the dead
and stinking innocently in the ditch.
A man had pushed that rod of his
between his legs between her legs.
Her skin slumped through her bones. She lay
in her own liquid filth licking
a piece of wood for succulence.
One morning she forgot her mother.
The winter froze two fingers off.
But milk and schoolsong recollections
kept her tough: she trusted God.
At last her turn she reached the ditch,
she knelt, was shot, fell blood to blood,
another elbow slapped across her neck.

I trembled safe across an ocean.
Behind the barbed roses of Connecticut
El Sereno boomed his "all is well."
I could not find, oh Stevens, syntax
for this child, no jewel adequate,
no shape of nature that would tally
or be wholesome (since through rock
and thorn and tiger, symbol-making man
can anodyne his grief). And ever
untranscended, pain stands by,
there is no exile into peace:
still on my lips that excrement
successors will digest to art
but I must suffer brute and fat,
clotting paradise out of my voice.

Notes. Orfèvres: jewelers. El sereno: a night-watchman in Spain.

AFTER HERRICK

swiftly the apple born   the apple praised
                the apple rotten
                swiftly we two
                    we too
                  forgotten

AFTER BABETTE DEUTSCH: *"The great lack of our time is that we have no commanding myth to which we can give allegiance."*

That Eve with snake made brisk alliance
was honest postlapsarian science.
Eden would have had small sale
as a cautionary tale.

Nor was it myth but rigid truth
that Atlas' girls were each a star,
though helium suits a star as well
in honesty's late avatar.

And Christ was fact, and Attis fact;
there was, but never is, a myth.
If gods were killed to grow the corn,
we've pumps and pipes to do it with.

Are they too bleak, the bonds of nitrogen?
Our sons will sigh for time was when
an atom hung from every eave,
and men were happy for they could believe.

AFTER GOETHE

Homunculus, son of the ocean
where the molecules arub-arub
make birth, where Venus and where God, maieutic,
    brood,
Homunculus swam for the dry when he grew up:

Thought, "Loved the plankton, algae, clams, and loved
the carp and loved the lurid Galatea last;"
and thought, "Upon the pebbles, shingles, flint,
Homunculus the chaste Homunculus shall fast."

Scandalized, a wave kicked him ashore
where Helen bathed; who blushed, but was not cold.
Homunculus forgot; he kissed her tit for tat,
he stayed the fool that heaven had foretold.

Ah Theseus, Jason, Menelaus, friends,
Venerically still the story ends.

Note. See *Faust*, Part II, especially scenes IV and V.

AFTER ROBERT FROST: *"I'd as soon make love in Lover's Lane as write for little magazines."*

If, dear sir, I hadn't saved my dollars in a roll
to pay a landlord's toll
for neatly swept surburban flat,
and if, dear friend, I didn't own a welcome mat
and two Kandinskys (copies to be sure),
a living-room with walnut furniture,
and nougats for my honey in a silver dish,
and furthermore a kitchen with a niche
where two can breakfast on Bavarian ware
(if it so happens two are there),
and had I not a confidential bed
with linen sheets and quilted coverlet,
a rug for pretty naked feet,
a burner with ecstatic heat,
and drapes to baffle streetlamps when they come
(the boors) to see is anybody home —
if, in short, I couldn't love my mistress
respectably upon a mattress,
I'd do it (braving frost) cramped in Lover's Lane
between the dashboard and the window-pane,
and there I might beget at that
a bouncing, saintly and immortal brat.

The Poet

OVERTURE

With less than pride
and modest adoration
a fly and I
pursue the light,
although it hangs
out of a bulb,
burning middling bright.

YOURS TRULY, PH.D.

I cannot build the house where I'm alive.
I do not understand the car I run.
And when I flick my lamp don't ask me how
A turbine wires me respectful light.

I walk in unintelligible shoes
Across a bridge that hangs I don't know why.
I give my TV set a witless stare;
I turn the knob, my science ends.

I'm dumb to vinyl, spoons and bevatrons.
How do they make a nail? A submarine?
What moves the lungs that move my telephone?
I cannot build the house in which I thrive.

But imbecile and talented I go,
Familiar, chipper, treading on your toe,

Blinking through the glasses I can't grind,
And more than glad to speak my parasitic mind.

WHEN IT RAINS I AM WET

When it rains I am wet
And when the sun shines I am dry:
I am no hero,
When the world hits I cry.

I am my harmony,
Choir of wishes,
But I do and die
As the bullet preaches.

FLOATING ROOM

I am not in the export and import line,
Nor in the professions; I am not a
Mechanical engineer; and I am not
The man who lubricates your car.
I live in a small apartment
On the twenty-seventh floor except
There are no stories underneath at all.
I am quite detached if you will allow
The pun and I do very little aside
From catching rain if it rains
With a butterfly net I stick out of my window;
Even the helicopters can't come
Very near because of the blades, and so
I will have to starve when the groceries
Run out but all things considered
I am not in the export and import line,
Nor in the professions; I am not a
Mechanical engineer; and I am not
The man who lubricates your car.

BLIND

The young man who is blind is smiling
while one reads the news to him.
He listens to the voice's voice,
pretends an interest in the din.

And when one leads him for a walk,
the tramways kneel politely;
he smiles like canny Moses
securing the Red Sea.

Taxes bend his neighbors, plutonium spills
and terrorists rap at my door.
He chats, he does not note
his cousins' blood slung on the floor.

And all the peevish race heaves
bread out of the earth, but one
comes feeding him, and still he smiles,
for he outwits the plan.

The wicked hate the wicked,
the kindlier hate the kind,
but he enacts the lamb
in the lion's arms reclined.

MON SEMBLABLE, MON FRÈRE

Praise-me-praise-me built the Parthenon
and peeled electrons shell by shell by shell.
But who invented praise-me-praise-me?
Lucifer or Gabriel?

Grass rhymes selflessly with grass,
winds, anonymous, mold cumuli.
Call it fine or call it foul:
mankind made its bed, and there I lie.

TO EMILY DICKINSON

I know you. Could we tell
the grass that you're made queen
(and king too) since you died,
and fibre pass the theme,

an underground of you
would feel the compliment,
and we should find some ease
because of compensation sent.

THE VISION OF JESUS OF NAZARETH
CONCERNING JOHANN SEBASTIAN BACH

Why do I carry this wooden cross so sunnily upon my
    back
And why do I suffer the little children to grin thornily
And my nakedness to be seen, and my flesh, oh Simon,
My body to be crucified under my father's smile
(Simon I dread the nails for all my soul's solidity)

And why am I who am the cause of cause
Dirtily dying for a dirty breed?
I am in canon with my future. I suffer
But I dwell upon my echo. Wipe my eyes.
The harpsichordist is beginning. I am safe.

WHO'S DIPHILUS?

Who's Diphilus? His works are lost.
He was a poet, won
some prizes, dented time
in Greece among the better men,

And got thrown out one time because
he wrote a stupid comedy.
Ten scholars now remember him;
that too is immortality.

OBADIAH HEAPE IS RECEIVED AT THE WHITE HOUSE AND APOLOGIZES TO HIS FELLOW-POETS

This is the world, and this the grave ass, man.
I made a book: Is and Should, Chaos and Plan
Like Vulcan lame with rage I banged
Into a shape for gods and men to understand.
The Nation was (it happened) looking out
For some great virtuous beast to boast about.
A busy President got wind, sent me a note
He wished to hang a medal on my coat.
I ran, and grinned, and had my photo snapped.
I spoke: the President looked rapt.
I lunched with senators and journalists.
I beamed each time my rump was kissed.
But then, Democritus, what can one say?
When mules are mighty, lions bray.

PERENNIALS
("Late Frost" by Suzuhiko Kawasaki)

A girl who faces away,
some loitering trees;
each stands alone
in a silver of snow.

The trees are undressed.
Looking their way
she guesses the old notion
that nothing is home.

Truths stiff with age
stir when their masters call.
Snow shivers again, again
a child cries in a wood.

In other spaces
be other calipers.
Here, the brush tips in
that most resilient cry . . .

Note. I purchased this painting from the artist in Tokyo in 1954.

TOM FIDDLE IN A HEAVENLY MOOD

I tiptoed on the daybreak of my genius
Saying to my very face, My God,

Tiptoed on the pinpoint of a blade
That spouted on the hill below the air,

One elbow on the sun and bussing
Winds to five incontinents,

Emitting jokes and raving holidays
And dating carnivals on Mondays —

Then do you know? the falcons turned herbivorous
And from a falling bomb mid-air

A chickadee came out and giggled
As it parachuted on a dying general,

And I employed the idle Angels
And hollered the Dominions to the job

Of shooting roasts of pigeon to the poor
In Togo and in Bangladesh —

Oh that was Sunday of my giant genius
And my name that Sunday was Your Grace

Serenity and Harlequin and never
Old Tom Fiddle with the wooden leg.

FRESH AIR

I am tired of the grapes and lilies
(Nature, take me dumb)
of "mist lifting out of brown cattails" —
of winds' "contorted strength" — of "pink rice
grains" meaning stars — of "undinal vast belly"
of the sea — and all such annotations.
Nature, take me dumb:
the bees and leaves have been recited,
my own life must be run.

I am tired of the topic love
(Woman, love me dumb)
of "willow eyelids" — of "intense fragility" —
twin breasts "cooing like doves under the eaves" —
or thighs "like papal marble" — and moans
for love's regrettable delinquencies.
Woman, love me dumb:
though eyes may be "deeper than roses,"
I am stark me and young.

Note. The quotations are all, I believe, from Marianne Moore.

SIR TOBY BELCH AGAINST SHAKESPEARE

"Poet, poet, tell me true,
What's the finest thing a man can do?"

      "Sow the verb and noun the earth,
      Fill the pen, and let the pen give birth."

"What of ladies and tycoons,
Gunshots, birds, tennis and saloons?"

      "A woman is a trochee at her best,
      A financier's an anapest,

      The bird is half a foot,
      And that's the use to which a bird is put."

"Farewell, grand master of the jingling craft.
Plato was no fool, who called you daft.

Your he she it what why and who
Get on and never think of you.

And I too swear no word can be
Better than a plump entelechy.

So I'll choose love, and even money,
And you can sing hey nonny nonny."

BO FU DECIDES TO STUDY THE BOOK OF PENTAGRAMS

Love I did, with tooth and tongue,
And sing I did, squalls of crotchets,
Blithe I lazed with tranquil eye,
Autumns flared and winters blazed,
And while their winds dissolved the trees
   I took the hours from a bonbonnière,
    And when the box was empty, found a spare.

But let me face the glorious facts:
Man is solid soul, he strives
To breathe with nostrils of a god,
He longs to task his deathless mind
And vaunt his distance from the beast.
   Besides, the lazy get no bread,
    And man must think in order to be fed.

The birdies fiddle sol mi do mi do.
But have they consciousness, the birdies? No.

Notes. Bu Fu is the unemployed sage of my *Chi Po and the Sorcerer.*
   Bonbonnière: candy-box.

A BAD DAY FOR POETRY

I loved you quaintly at the verge of a kiss.
Poet, the wind blew, was killed in July,
And dropped me in the sun. Nothing is complete.
I have no texts, only some indices.

God wiped his mouth, nudged his dark Brother,
And said, pointing where Moses sweated:
"Show Moses the suburb of Palestine,
And shoot him at the border."

A BAD DAY FOR POETRY

Harder, my boy, harder the speech,
stiffer the thoughts that ought to bend,
emotion lengthens into bone,
love is gesture, blood is bleach.

The poems stick like glue or oil.
To me my cough sounds louder
than each bursting of the sorry stars.
My place is purchased in the soil.

A BAD DAY FOR POETRY

I was a child and when I was,
I worded high and strong the gusty sun
Or sponged the seas into my verbs.

But I grew old and now I am,
Where are the green syllabic fields,
The night is thin, where is the child?

A BAD DAY FOR POETRY

The rhythms wobble and the words have quit.
My poetry must be desiring it.

A BAD DAY FOR POETRY

1
Like an old man who places
one foot before the other and figures
before he brings his other forward
before the first. So much for victory.
As for enthusiasms with regard to skies,
Fra Angelico, the touching bosoms of St. Tropez,
he hates three mammas who occupy his bench.

2

Time was, I launched asseverations.
I never thought but I encompassed.
I cried, five times a day: oh!

FRESH START

Hand to essence:
   the hair and pimple of fact
   and finger-cushion of the feel
(snatching a girl from her mate,
   or hanging my dog with a rope,
   or undrowning an ant:)
the do of do:

Mouth to essence:
   for instance death,
   the undo and the doneout of it:
   no paragraph to hint me how
it sucks me out of me:

Lung to essence:
   like a bare first man
   in undecoded jungle:
I hack through sugared grammars:
   back to thing: place my breathing
   where I pick:

Pushing my birth:
   I womb of I,
   white is my color in the world,
no dad no history:
   hungry trying sand
   and thirsty lapping gravel:
if I so will I will.

SHOULD

Like the tip of a stranger's tongue
in the corner of your eye
the poem
should

PIGEON FLY

What I have in my hand here
   is a pigeon my friends although
if it were whiter I should call it
   dove, which is more promising.

I am hardly Noah as I lean
   holding my pigeon at the window,
but as it's Spring and trees jump out
   and flap their leaves: pigeon, fly!

It does not fly as elegantly
   as in pictures I have seen;
still, it bears that little paper tube
   tied round its ankle for my heirs.

How curious it will be, the day
   they open it and nothing's written there.
"What made him send that stupid bird?"
   when I so dead cannot reply.

FAREWELL

Drink, my gullibles,
drink the decanter dry
where truth ferments
to savory lie.

Christ barked his orders,
the gospel sings.
Let us pretend
we have wings.

FAREWELL

Le Roi Soleil struck down his man
by looking through his face
as though it were a spot of air
hung in a vacant space.

The world has done with me
entirely the same;
I could not even draw
the compliment of blame.

Come silence and farewell.
I'll never kiss
a word's lips with another rhyme:
the last be this.

EPILOGUE

My pen you see roves little in the world,
my syllables are monks. For I perceive
that rhyming warm or cold won't hang a rascal
by the feet nor at the crisis shackle
any raving general. Mine the grief
that trails the earthworm to its punctual bird;
mine the minute dominion of the self:
dominion neither Guibelline nor Guelf.